Michelangelo

BY KLAUS OTTMANN

THE WONDERLAND
PRESS

Harry N. Abrams, Inc., Publishers

THE WONDERLAND PRESS

The Essential™ is a trademark
of The Wonderland Press, New York
The Essential™ series has been created by The Wonderland Press

Series Producer: John Campbell
Series Editor: Harriet Whelchel
Project Manager: Adrienne Moucheraud
Series Design: The Wonderland Press

Library of Congress Control Number: 00–105484
ISBN 0-7407-0728-0 (Andrews McMeel)
ISBN 0-8109-5817-1 (Harry N. Abrams, Inc.)

On the end pages: David (detail). 1501–4. Marble
Galleria dell'Accademia, Florence

All images of the Sistine Chapel are © Nippon Television Network Corporation

Printed in Hong Kong

Harry N. Abrams, Inc.
100 Fifth Avenue
New York, NY 10011
www.abramsbooks.com

PHOTOGRAPHY CREDITS:
Alinari 4; Nicolo Orsi Battaglini 103; Erich Lessing 20, 68, 78; Nimatallah 69, 104;
Scala 17, 22, 25, 36, 39, 40, 41, 44, 45, 47, 51, 65, 66, 71, 75, 77, 80, 81, 92, 93, 96, 97,
101, 107, end pages

Contents

What's in a Name?

Some people are so famous they're known by one name only. Take Cher, Armani, and Picasso, for example. Or Michelangelo, the genius sculptor, painter, architect, and poet whose name epitomizes all that was splendid about 16th-century Italian art. If Michelangelo were alive today, no doubt his name (and perhaps the image of his erotic statue *David*) would be licensed to purveyors of fine clothing, leather bags, chic marble, ceiling paint, and endless variations of high-end accessories and low-end tschotskies (think *David* refrigerator magnets shaped in the form of his body). In short, the artist known as "Il divino Michelangelo" would be a hot item at today's A-list parties, on *Oprah* and other talk shows, and in the homes of the rich and famous.

OPPOSITE
One of the four nudes who surround the prophet Jeremiah in the Fresco on the ceiling of the Sistine Chapel 1508–12

Sound Byte:
"If a man is called to be a street sweeper, he should sweep streets even as Michelangelo painted, or Beethoven composed music, or Shakespeare wrote poetry. He should sweep streets so well that all the hosts of heaven and earth will pause to say, he lived."

—MARTIN LUTHER KING, JR. (1929–1968),
U.S. civil rights leader, clergyman

Sound Byte:

> *"An absolute Superman."*
>
> —HENRY MOORE, British sculptor, on Michelangelo, 1966

Why the Attraction to Michelangelo?

During the 1964 New York World's Fair, thousands of people waited anxiously to see Michelangelo's heartbreakingly beautiful masterpiece, *Pietà*, a sculpture in marble and one of the world's most famous works of art. This would be the only time that the sculpture, an exquisite rendering of the body of Christ draped across the lap of a grieving Madonna, could be seen outside of Italy. Since the public is not known for going wild over marble sculptures or statues, what is it about Michelangelo's creations that inspires such awe?

For starters, his work is filled with sexy nude bodies. Michelangelo defied the laws of gravity and of physics every time he turned a block of marble into a living entity, each time he "freed" the subject of his sculpture from a block of struggling, resistant ("recalcitrant") marble. He was an early example of a PR maven and self-promoting artist. Like such celebrated artists as **Pablo Picasso** (1881–1973), **Andy Warhol** (1928–1987), and **Salvador Dalí** (1904–1989), he took an active role in the creation of his own cult of personality.

Did you know that Michelangelo:

- was one of the three major stars of what is now called the "High Renaissance" (**Leonardo da Vinci** and **Raphael** were the other two);

- was the most technically accomplished sculptor since classical antiquity;

- raised to extraordinary new lengths the standard for sculpting the nude;

- achieved an unprecedented unity between painting, sculpture, and architecture?

Daniele de Volterra
Portrait of Michelangelo
(detail). c. 1548–53
Black chalk. 9'3" x 7'2"
(295 x 219 cm)

The Times, they were a' changing: the Renaissance (1410–1600)

So what was the Renaissance anyway? The term *renaissance* is French for *rebirth* and describes the radical changes that took place in European art and culture during the 15th and 16th centuries. The Renaissance began in Italy in the 15th century when Florence was the center of artistic activity. It stood as the bridge between the Middle Ages and the beginning of the modern age of art and civilization as we know them. It was characterized by the spirit of artistic individuality, an exuberance for the arts and sciences, and a rediscovery of ancient Greek and Roman culture, which gave rise to the idea of *humanism,* which focused on humans and their abilities. It was a time of great geographical exploration and interest in scientific inquiry. Renaissance artists introduced the idea of *perspective* into painting, a method of representing the three-dimensional world on a two-dimensional surface by using a single vanishing point to which all lines on a pictorial surface recede.

OPPOSITE
Expulsion
Fresco on
the ceiling
Sistine Chapel
1508–12
(295 x 219 cm)

Although the term *Italian Renaissance* generally refers to an entire period of art and culture, historians traditionally divide it into three phases, even if the dates are somewhat arbitrary:

The **Early Renaissance** began in Florence in 1410–20 and developed over a period of several decades. It was characterized by the introduction of linear perspective, proportion, *contrapposto* (see BACKTRACK on page 26), and a return to the classical nude, although this return fell short of

9

a realistic representation of the human figure. The Early Renaissance was inspired by the humanism of the 14th century and is thought to have found its first expression in the architecture of **Filippo Brunelleschi** (1377–1446); in the paintings of **Masaccio** (1401–1428), **Domenico Ghirlandaio** (1449–1494), and **Sandro Botticelli** (c. 1444–1510); and in the sculptures of **Donato Donatello** (1386–1466).

The **High Renaissance** began in 1495 and ended with the death of the artist Raphael in 1520. It was characterized by a unification of pictorial or architectural composition, and by the balancing of all elements toward a more naturalistic representation. Its main proponents were **Leonardo da Vinci** (1452–1519), **Raphael** (1483–1520), **Titian** (c. 1488–1576), and of course **Michelangelo** (1475–1564).

Sound Byte:
> *"Genius is eternal patience."*
> —MICHELANGELO

The **Late Renaissance** overlapped with the High Renaissance and with the style known as *Mannerism* (see BACKTRACK on page 83), and ended around 1600. It valued grace and elegance, and was represented by the later works of Michelangelo, as well as by those of the painters **Paolo Veronese** (1528–1588) and **Tintoretto** (1518–1594).

Michelangelo's Italy

The 15th century was a period of great exploration by Spanish, Portuguese, and Italian seafarers (recall: the year 1492 marked the discovery of the New World by Christopher Columbus). During this time, Italian cities were allowed a high degree of autonomy and they often expanded their political influence over the surrounding regions. In Michelangelo's time, the name *Italy* was rarely used when speaking of the country itself.

The country was part of the Holy Roman Empire ruled by **Emperor Maximilian** (1493–1519). It was not a democracy, but rather was made up of 14 separate republics, kingdoms, feudal townships, and *city-states*, which were individual regions ruled by petty tyrants or by a single wealthy family or group of families, and which were often at war with one another. (To grasp the notion of city-states, imagine an America where individual states such as Indiana or Georgia were independent entities that were not part of the union of the United States and that rivaled each other for power and control over each other.)

The most powerful states during the 15th and 16th centuries were the republics of Venice and Florence, the papal states ruled by the pope in Rome (back then, he was an absolute political ruler with enormous military power), the kingdom of Naples, and the duchy of Milan.

Ah, power!

OPPOSITE
Detail of
*Madonna
and Child*
(aka *Medici
Madonna*)
1521
Marble
Height 8'3"
(252.7 cm)
with base
Medici Chapel, San Lorenzo
Florence

Renaissance society consisted essentially of five classes, listed here from highest to lowest: (1) the old nobility; (2) the capitalist and banker classes; (3) the merchants and tradespeople; (4) the poor; and (5) the domestic slaves (the Italian Renaissance was the first modern society to reinstitute slavery).

Since the Italian Renaissance was a period of continuous internal political conflicts between the numerous city-states, the only way to secure a territory was to form alliances with untrustworthy powers in order to keep a watchful eye on them. This delicate balance of power was interrupted several times, most dramatically when Italy was invaded by the French in 1495. The pope had betrayed Milan by allowing Naples to invade the duchy, and the French invasion came about when the ruler of Milan struck an alliance with France after the pope's betrayal. Because of this ongoing political agitation, Italy's states and republics were in a constant state of military defense throughout the Renaissance, threatened in the north by France and in the south by Spain, as well as by various intrigues and military strikes from within.

Located in the heart of Tuscany, about 145 miles northwest of Rome, Florence achieved preeminence in commerce, banking, and the arts between the 14th and 16th centuries. It was the birthplace of the Italian Renaissance and produced some of Italy's greatest minds, such as the

artists **Leonardo da Vinci**, the poet **Dante Alighieri** (1265–1321), the philosopher **Niccolò Machiavelli** (1469–1527), the astronomer **Galileo Galilei** (1564–1642), the explorer **Amerigo Vespucci** (1454–1512), and, of course, Michelangelo.

The Medici Family

While Florence was nominally a republic, it was ruled during most of the Renaissance by members of the powerful **Medici** family, whose banking empire consisted of branches in London, Paris, Rome, Venice, and elsewhere. Just as the silent-film star Norma Desmond proclaimed in the movie *Sunset Boulevard*, "Without me, there would be no Paramount Studio," one might argue that without the Medici as bene-factors, there would be no Michelangelo. The Medici were important sources of capital to kings, foreign governments, the Holy Roman Emperor, and the pope. They were passionate collectors of art and surrounded themselves with vibrant, creative people who formed the fabric of Florentine civilization. Even though the Medici were the de facto rulers of Florence, they respected the principles of republican government and were careful to respect the Signoria, the city's governing body (of course, it consisted of elected members who were, for the most part, supporters of the Medici family).

The family rose to prominence with the brilliant and wise **Cosimo de' Medici** (1388–1464), who was succeeded by his son **Piero**

de' Medici, known as Piero the Gouty because of his arthritis. Upon Piero's death in 1469, **Lorenzo de' Medici** (1449–1492), at the age of 20, became the leader of the family. When we think of the heyday of the Medici family, with their philanthropy and generosity toward artists and the culture of Florence, it is Lorenzo—known as "the Magnificent"—who comes to mind. More than any other Medici, Lorenzo personified the Renaissance spirit and devotion to the joys of Greek and Roman culture. A diplomat and a gentleman, he loved the people of Florence and respected their need for independence from tyranny. For this, he was much loved by the citizens, who found him friendly and approachable.

Lorenzo held lively and witty meetings of friends and scholars to discuss the arts, literature, culture, and the sciences. They shared a love for the Greek philosopher **Plato** (427–347 B.C.) and the Platonic idea of the human body as the visible aspect of the soul. This joyous pursuit of things cultural by Lorenzo and his friends would play an important role in the artistic formation of the young Michelangelo.

Hotline to Michelangelo

How come we know so much about Michelangelo? In part, because he left behind hundreds of letters, sketches, and poems, but also because his career was more fully documented during his lifetime than that of any artist of his time or before him. Michelangelo was the first living

Giorgio Vasari
Self-Portrait
(detail). 1566–68
Oil on wood. 39 ⁵/₈ x 31 ¹/₂"
(100.5 x 80 cm)

artist to see his biography published during his lifetime (*The Lives of the Most Excellent Painters, Sculptors, and Architects*). It appeared in 1550 and was the work of **Giorgio Vasari** (1511–1574), a close friend and pupil of Michelangelo's, and a painter and architect in his own right (he designed the Uffizi Palace in Florence). Vasari's writings as an art historian remain the single most important source of our knowledge about Michelangelo and, by extension, about Renaissance art. Vasari was essentially the first publicist of the Italian Renaissance.

It's all in the Milk

And so the story begins: The future artist **Michelangelo di Lodovico Buonarroti** was born on March 6, 1475 (a Pisces!), in Caprese, a small town 40 miles south of Florence, Italy. He was the second of five sons born to **Ludovico Buonarroti Simoni** and **Francesca del Neri**, minor aristocrats whose fortunes had declined since the Buonarroti family's prominence 200 years earlier. Apart from owning a small share in a house located in Florence and a tiny farm east of Florence in the stone-quarry village of Settignano, the Buonarrotis had nothing. The shallow, arrogant Ludovico begrudged the fact that his family no longer had the money or the

*Madonna of the
Stairs.* 1491
Marble
22 x 15 ³/₄"
(55.8 x 40 cm)

status that it once had, yet he continued to see himself as an aristocrat and refused to work as a merchant or farmer. Aristocrats, after all, were above that!

Francesca was young when the couple married and was soon exhausted from the demands of her self-centered husband. In late 1474, several months before Michelangelo was born, Ludovico received a six-month appointment as governor of Caprese and Chiusi, two remote villages east of Florence in the hill country. The small burgs were located high in the mountains, surrounded by choppy, rocky terrain and primitive roads that were barely passable. Ludovico and Francesca made the arduous journey with their 18-month-old son, **Lionardo**. The trip was all the more stressful for Francesca, since she was pregnant with Michelangelo. They finally reached the drafty, run-down castle where they would make their home for six months only, and on March 6, 1475, Michelangelo was born. A few weeks later, Ludovico's term as governor ended and the family moved back to Florence. Having once again made the difficult trip through the mountains, Michelangelo's mother was too frail to nurse him, so the infant was sent to Settignano, where he was placed with a wet nurse in a family of stonecutters. Giorgio Vasari, the biographer, would later write that *Michelangelo took the hammer and chisels from his wet-nurse's milk*. Only on rare occasions did the child return to Florence to visit his family.

Michelangelo's mother died when the boy was six years old. Four years later, after his father had remarried, Michelangelo was sent back to live with his family in Florence. For the first time, he briefly attended school, though he had no interest in reading and writing. He had spent several years in Settignano learning the craft of stonecutting and his heart was already set on art. Despite his father's protests, the child frequently skipped classes to go out and look at the abundance of statues and paintings throughout Florence. Although he gradually picked up a little Greek and Latin, it was art and drawing that obsessed Michelangelo, and he spent many hours copying the figures from paintings and sculptures that he saw in churches and in public buildings.

During this time, Michelangelo had the good fortune to become a friend of the artist **Francesco Granacci** (1477–1543), who was six years older and who was already apprenticed to the Florentine painter **Domenico del Ghirlandaio** (1449–1494). Ghirlandaio's workshop, a busy, thriving enterprise, had a large staff of assistants and apprentices who created altarpieces for churches, portraits for prominent citizens, furniture with scenes from the Bible, and so on. Through Granacci,

Michelangelo made the acquaintance of artists and wonderfully eccentric people, and from that moment on he knew where he wanted to be.

Entranced by the idea of quitting school and becoming an apprentice to Ghirlandaio, Michelangelo begged his father to arrange for an apprenticeship. Ludovico, of course, would hear nothing of this, since he considered artists lower than shoemakers. Moreover, he wanted Michelangelo to make lots of money and help restore the family's status as thriving, affluent aristocrats.

But Michelangelo stood firm and bulldozed through his father's resistance. On April 1, 1488, at the age of 13, he left school for good and, with the begrudging consent of his father, signed up for an apprenticeship in Ghirlandaio's workshop. Finally, he had entered the world of the arts, where he not only felt he belonged, but where his future would begin to take shape.

In the summer of 1489, a near-miracle happened in the 14-year-old's life. Lorenzo's people asked Ghirlandaio to suggest the names of possible interns who could assist the sculptor **Bertoldo di Giovanni** in maintaining the Medici collection of Greek and Roman sculptures in the Gardens of San Marco, located near the Medici

The Louvre, Paris

Domenico Ghirlandaio
*Portrait of an Old Man
and a Boy.* c. 1480–90
Oil on panel. 24 ³/₈ x 18 ¹/₈"
(62 x 46.1 cm)

palace. Michelangelo was selected as one of Bertoldo's pupils and immediately left Ghirlandaio's workshop. While working with Bertoldo, he was "discovered" by Lorenzo de' Medici and invited to live as his protégé in the Medici palace, along with other talented young artists, who were welcomed as family. Michelangelo studied with the Medici children, some of whom would later become popes.

> **FYI: How Michelangelo broke his nose**—During his time at the Medici sculpture garden, the young Michelangelo made fun of a fellow student, the sculptor Pietro Torrigiano, who was known for his terrible temper. Bad idea! Torrigiano punched him in the nose, and since cosmetic surgery as we know it had not yet been invented, Michelangelo was disfigured for life.

First Works

In 1491, while living in Lorenzo's palace, Michelangelo executed a marble *relief*, or plaque, entitled *Madonna of the Stairs* (see page 17). The work displays the artist's astonishing mastery of the delicate marble techniques of the 15th-century sculptors and his immersion in the classical art from the sculptures in the Medici Gardens. An image of complete solitude, which will also appear in Michelangelo's later figures, his *Madonna* depicts the Virgin absorbed in her thoughts as she foresees the death of her child. However, the vagueness of the human figure and

Casa Buonarroti, Florence.

the almost certain inaccuracies in the perspective of the stairway to heaven reveal it as the work of a beginner.

A year later, he completed *Battle of the Centaurs*, a small, shallow marble relief inspired by the tradition of classical Roman battle scenes. (Centaurs were the half-human, half-horse figures in Greek mythology.) The crowded relief gives an astonishing foretaste of his mature ability to unfold passion and tragedy through the dense interaction of nude bodies. Already there are signs of his later Mannerist style, in particular the nudes in his monumental *The Last Judgment*, part of the fresco art in the Sistine Chapel (see page 82). *Battle of the Centaurs* was a work to which Michelangelo felt a lifelong attachment, and he is said to have kept it on the walls of his studio throughout his life.

Learning from the Dead

Tragically, the beloved Lorenzo died on April 8, 1492, at the age of 43. He had been ill for several weeks, but his death came as a blow to his fellow citizens, and especially to Michelangelo, who now found himself without a mentor. The artist had no choice but to return to live in his father's house in Florence. Lorenzo's oldest

OPPOSITE
Battle of the Centaurs
c. 1492. Marble
33 ¹/₄ x 33 ⁵/₈" (85 x 90 cm)

BELOW
Death Mask of Lorenzo the Magnificent. 1492

son, **Piero de' Medici** (1471–1503), "the Unlucky One," was chosen by the Signoria to become first citizen of the republic. But his arrogance kept him from evolving into the adept leader that his father had been for 23 years, and his lack of respect for the Florentines' independence would prove to be his undoing.

While living with his father, Michelangelo received an invitation from the prior of the monastery of Santo Spirito (which the Medici had long supported) to observe the dissection of corpses and to study the anatomy of the human body. Unlike his rival, Leonardo da Vinci, Michelangelo was interested in anatomy not because of scientific curiosity but because he wished to capture the human figure accurately in his art.

In exchange for the monastery's allowing him to spend time in the morgue, Michelangelo produced his only wooden carving, a *Crucifix* (c. 1492–93) for the monastery. Happily, it was rediscovered nearly five centuries later, in 1962, but had been heavily overpainted throughout the years.

Like most 15th-century crucifixes made during Michelangelo's time, it would have been ornately decorated with a crown of real thorns. It was the first crucifix in the Renaissance to feature the body of Christ in a *contrapposto* pose. (See BACKTRACK on page 26.)

BACKTRACK:
CONTRAPPOSTO

Contrapposto is Italian for *opposite*. The concept originated with the ancient Greek sculptors, who knew that the weight of a statue rests on one leg and that this freed the other leg so that it could bend at the knee and cause the hips, shoulders, and head to tilt. In the Renaissance, this scheme was taken to a more sophisticated level by a more intimate knowledge of human anatomy. Michelangelo dramatized the tilting effect by forcing the head and legs in opposite directions, as he did in the *Santo Spirito Crucifix*, or by pushing one arm forward over a receding leg, as he did in *David*.

Keeping your Clients happy

When in 1493 a rare blizzard in Florence produced unusual amounts of snow, Michelangelo conceded to a request by Piero de' Medici to carve a snowman in the middle of the Medici palace courtyard. This was not an unusual request: Renaissance artists were routinely asked to create temporary decorations for the entertainment of their rich patrons. Piero was so pleased with Michelangelo's snow sculpture that he invited him to stay again in the palace for several months.

From the Medici to Savonarola

Piero, alas, was a weak leader and, in October 1494, the French king Charles VIII invaded Naples, an ally of Florence. Piero panicked and surrendered Florence's fortifications to the French. Chaos erupted in the Tuscan city and Piero fled, never to return. This political unrest proved to be the end of the 60-year reign of the Medici family, at least for the time being. Their palace was ransacked, the streets were stormed by angry mobs, and the serenity of happier days was but a memory, replaced by a new republican regime.

Who was Girolamo Savonarola?

With Piero gone, the Florentine government was taken over by a fanatical prior of the Dominican monastery of San Marco in Florence named **Girolamo Savonarola** (1452–1498), who believed that he had been sent by God to warn people of impending doom. When the Medici were banished from Florence in 1494 and anarchy ruled the city, Savonarola's People's Party won in a landslide the first election under the new democratic constitution. Christ was declared the King of Florence and all "sinful" activities, including horse racing, gambling, and prostitution, were severely penalized.

Fearing for his safety, as a protégé of the Medici family, Michelangelo fled to Venice in late 1494 and then to Bologna, where he was taken in by the aristocratic magistrate **Gianfrancesco Aldovrandi**, who helped him obtain a commission for sculpting three figures for the magnificent tomb of St. Dominic, the founder of the Dominican order of monks. Work had begun on the tomb in 1265 and over the years various sculptors had worked on it. Michelangelo's additions to it included the statuettes of *St. Proclus* (1494–95) and *St. Petronius* (1494–95), and a kneeling *Angel* (1494–95), who holds

Basilica of San Domenico, Bologna, Italy

St. Proclus
1494–95. Marble
Height 24" (58.5 cm)

27

a hefty candelabrum. None of these figures is more than about two feet high, but they were important commissions, in part because the military *St. Proclus* is thought to foreshadow *David*.

A Case of Forgery

Even though life with Aldovrandi was pleasant, Michelangelo was homesick for Florence, so, in the winter of 1495, he returned to the city that Piero de' Medici had unsuccessfully attempted to recapture. Once there, he was commissioned by **Lorenzo di Pier Francesco de' Medici** (1463–1507), a cousin of Lorenzo the Magnificent and a member of the "Republican" Medici clan (i.e., the branch of the family that had aligned itself with the newly formed republican government), to carve a marble statue of a youthful *John the Baptist* and a small marble *Sleeping Cupid* (both lost). When Lorenzo di Pier Francesco saw the latter, he suggested to Michelangelo that it would bring more money if it looked as if it were an authentic antique. Michelangelo promptly buried the statue in the ground for some time to make it appear old, and the *Sleeping Cupid* was sold as an antique through an intermediary art dealer to **Cardinal Raffaelo Riario** (1461–1521) of San Giorgio, a major Roman art collector and one of the most influential men in Rome. Although the cardinal paid the unscrupulous dealer 200 ducats for it, Michelangelo received only 30.

Eventually the cardinal learned that the sculpture was a fake and sent an investigator to find the artist who had done the forgery. When the cardinal's emissary confronted Michelangelo, the latter offered to refund the money he had been paid in return for the statue. Cardinal Riario realized that it was the dealer, not Michelangelo, who had been dishonest and was able to obtain a refund of his 200 ducats from the dealer. When the dealer received the sculpture from the cardinal, he immediately sold it to another client, so Michelangelo was unable to reacquire the piece for himself. It was never considered an "art forgery" in the present sense, since it was a great achievement for any artist at the time to be able to carve marble as well as the Greeks and Romans had done. (Footnote: In the 1630s, the statue ended up in the possession of the English King Charles I and was later destroyed in a fire.)

Men helping men

The upside of this melodrama was that Michelangelo became a friend of Cardinal Riario. And since there was little to do in Florence, Michelangelo accepted the cardinal's offer to live and work in Rome, the city commanded by the papacy. The sitting pope at the time of Michelangelo's arrival in 1496 was the Spaniard Rodrigo Borgia, known as **Pope Alexander VI**, whose term lasted from 1492 until 1503.

Promptly after his arrival in Rome, Michelangelo carved a larger-than-life, richly sensual statue of *Bacchus* (1496–98), the Roman god of wine, for the cardinal. The sculptor took great pains to model his statue after

Bacchus
1496–97. Marble
Height 80"
(203. cm)

classical antiquities, and in *Bacchus* he explored the forms of human flesh in a manner unprecedented since ancient times. The free-standing statue actually consists of two figures: a small grape-stealing satyr and a reeling, drunken Bacchus.

Evidently, the cardinal wasn't fond of the sculpture; in his view, *Bacchus* did not measure up to the standards of the Greek and Roman statues in Riario's collection. Instead of finding a home with Riario, the statue was moved in 1497 to the collection of the Roman banker, **Jacopo Galli**, who became the artist's main patron in Rome. A 1530s drawing of Galli's sculpture garden by one of Michelangelo's contemporaries shows that the statue was already missing its penis, which Michelangelo had purposely broken off in order to increase the classical effect.

Galli rocks!

Galli and Michelangelo developed an unusually strong relationship, the details of which are known only sketchily. He commissioned the sculptor to create a new *Cupid*, which has also disappeared. But he also became Michelangelo's financial guarantor, cosigning loans for him and guaranteeing collateral for the sculptor's increasing investments. It was Galli who, on August 29, 1498, negotiated the contract between Michelangelo and **Cardinal Jean Bilhère de Lagraulas**, the elderly French emissary to the papal court who was getting ready to retire and move home to France. The cardinal wanted to commission a monument in St. Peter's, the papal cathedral in the Vatican, in Rome. He decided that the marble sculpture should feature the Virgin with the dead Christ, a subject known as *Pietà* (Italian for *pity*). It would become the most important work of Michelangelo's early career.

Sound Byte:

"I, Jacopo Galli, pledge my word to his most reverent lordship that the said Michelangelo will finish the said work within one year, and that it shall be the finest work in marble which Rome today can show, and that no master of our days shall be able to produce a better one."

—From Michelangelo's contract for the *Pietà*, 1498

More Mischief from Savonarola

While Michelangelo was still in Rome, Savonarola, in his ongoing crusade against sin and evil, was alleging that the papacy had become corrupted by Satan. He preached against luxury and corruption and organized public "bonfires of the vanities" in front of the Palace of the Signoria during which he exhorted the citizens of Florence to burn any nonreligious belongings, including works of art. The citizens of Florence had grown weary of his tirades, and decided that he had crossed the line of unacceptable behavior when he denounced Pope Alexander VI as the "Antichrist." The independent-minded Florentines sought the pope's backing to have Savonarola arrested, and in 1498, he was hanged, stoned, and burned in the center of the Piazza della Signoria in Florence.

Turning Point: the *Pietà*

With Savonarola gone, Michelangelo could easily have returned to Florence, but he opted to remain in Rome in order to pursue the *Pietà* (1498–99). He began the sculpture by traveling to the marble quarries in Carrara to select a piece of marble. At the quarries, blocks of marble were cut by chiseling a groove into a vein of the stone, then inserting wedges of olive wood, and pouring water on them. The expanding wedges would split the marble along the groove. Secured by ropes and slings, the blocks would then be hauled onto carts. Before the blocks were transported to Rome, Michelangelo would mark them and make detailed and annotated sketches of them, which he would then have notarized as proofs of ownership.

After the marble had been selected, Michelangelo began the sculpture by carving a lifesize clay model. Its proportions would then be transferred to the marble block with the help of a mechanical device that consisted of a kind of "rotating ruler." First, the clay model would be measured in great detail. Then, its measurements would be transferred to the marble block. Before Michelangelo could transform the surface of the marble into sensuous, lifelike figures, his assistants, skilled stone carvers, would chip away at the marble with mallets and pointed chisels (which left the pockmarks visible on some of Michelangelo's unfinished sculptures). Next, he would employ toothed chisels to bring out more detail and then refine the surface with a smooth chisel. The final step would be the smoothing of the marble with files and rasps.

The *Pietà* depicts a seated Madonna holding the corpse of Christ across her knees, after His descent from the cross. The sculpture has unusual proportions: If the figures were to stand up, Mary would be more than 7' tall whereas Christ would be only 5'8" tall. Yet Mary's head is the same size as that of Christ.

The sculpture, an image of extreme restraint, invites us to contemplate Christ's sacrifice. Rather than displaying sorrow, Mary is shown in a meditative pose, her head lowered toward the dead body of her son. Michelangelo limits the expression of Mary's grief to her outstretched left hand, a gesture inspired by Leonardo da Vinci's depiction of Christ in *The Last Supper*. Michelangelo's delicate modeling of Christ's body transfers the warmth of Mary's living flesh to the cold marble, thus creating the impression of sleep rather than death.

FYI: On May 21, 1972, a vandal attacked the *Pietà* with a hammer. Mary's face was heavily damaged and her left arm broken off, but the statue has since been restored.

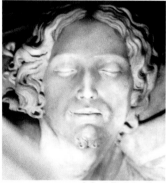

ABOVE
Detail of
the *Pietà*
Christ's face

RIGHT
Detail of
the *Pietà*
Head of
the Virgin

The *Pietà* is the only one of Michelangelo's sculptures that bears his signature in his own hand. Legend has it that one day after it had been installed, Michelangelo overheard a group of foreign visitors discussing the sculpture, which they assumed had been done by some other artist. To head off future misattribution, Michelangelo returned the following night with his tools to chisel his name in Latin into Mary's sash. The inscription reads *Michelangelus Buonarrotus Fiorentinus Faciebat* ("Michelangelo Buonarroti the Florentine made this"). His completion of the *Pietà* at the young age of 24 sealed Michelangelo's celebrity status in Rome.

Sound Byte:
"No sculptor, not even the most rare artist, could ever reach this level of design and grace, nor could he, even with hard work, ever finish, polish, and cut marble as skillfully as Michelangelo did here, for in this statue all of the worth and power of sculpture is revealed."
—GIORGIO VASARI, on Michelangelo's *Pietà*, 1568

Size does Matter: *David* (1501–4)

In 1501, Michelangelo returned to Florence, where the tyrannic regime of Savonarola had been replaced by a new central assembly, the Grand Council, a form of popular government that included 3,000 members. He had heard from a friend that the Committee of Works of the cathedral in Florence was interested in commissioning him to create an important sculpture. For 35 years, a huge, partially carved block of pure white Carrara marble had lain abandoned by an earlier sculptor, **Agostino di Duccio** (1418–1481), in the workyard of the cathedral in Florence. The Committee of Works (which included the painters Leonardo da Vinci and Sandro Botticelli) decided to invite sculptors to participate in a competition to create a statue to be carved out of the badly blocked-out stone. The project had become known as "the Giant."

In the end, they offered the Giant to the 26-year-old Michelangelo, in part because his was the only proposal that did not include new marble to be added to the existing block, but also because, a few years earlier, he had executed a larger-than-life statue of *Hercules* (which disappeared in 1713). Michelangelo had proposed a statue of the youthful biblical hero David, slayer of Goliath, as a kind of symbol of Florentine independence and defiance of tyranny. The Wool Guild, which made the final choice, liked his idea.

Michelangelo saw sculpture as the art of "taking away," not of "adding on": Whereas painters add paint to a canvas, sculptors remove marble from a block to "free" the form inside. Even in his unfinished statues, one can clearly see this process of taking away, or carving. Either the surfaces are complete, save for the final polishing, or they are concealed by the rough masses of the blocked-in marble. There is no intermediate stage.

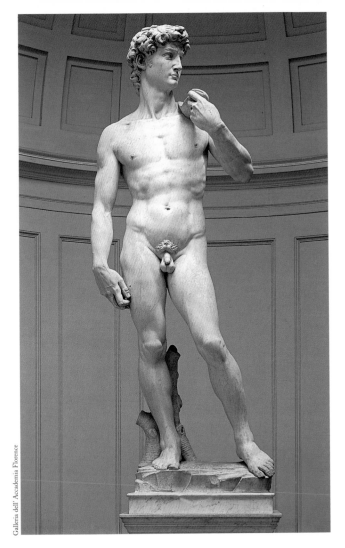

David
1501–4
Marble. Height
13' 6" (410 cm)
without base

David
seen from behind

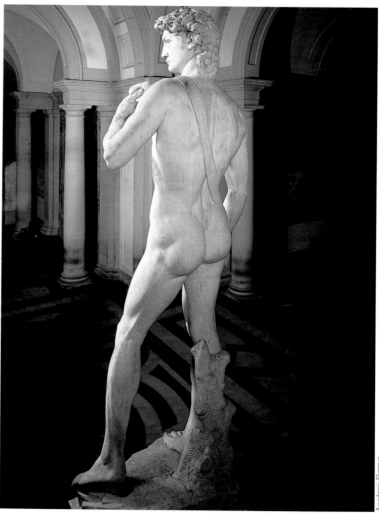

On September 13, 1501, Michelangelo began work on the colossal *David* and for the next two and a half years he would labor tirelessly with his chisels, rasps, hammers, and files. The crew had constructed a large wooden structure around the block of marble, with scaffolding that allowed him to maneuver his way around all parts of the huge block. Bit by bit, the marble chips fell in piles on the ground as the gigantic figure of David began to emerge from the block.

When the piece was completed and unveiled in September 1504, **it established Michelangelo as the greatest living sculptor in Italy** and dethroned Donatello's famous yet considerably shorter, boyish bronze statue *David*, which was no match for Michelangelo's beefy, sensual version of the Old Testament giant slayer. *David* became the first statement of the sculptor's mature genius. Together with Leonardo's painting *Mona Lisa*, was one of the first major works of the High Renaissance and represented the Platonic vision of the ideal youthful hero, along with the courage, vision, and awesome power that the Italians call *terribilità*.

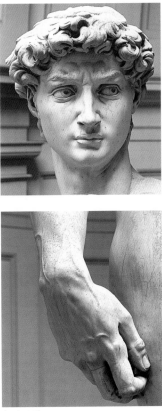

Accademia Florence

Details of *David*

Replica of *David* outside the Palazzo Vecchio. Marble Height 13' 6" (410 cm) Piazza della Signoria Florence

Although the statue was executed less than half a mile from the Palazzo Vecchio, it took four days and 40 men to move the finished piece on greased wooden beams to its final location. At night, the sculpture had to be guarded against stone throwers, who were angry about the statue's uncompromising nudity and also by its political symbolism. The original free-standing sculpture, which stands over 13' high and weighs roughly 11,000 pounds, was finally moved inside the Galleria dell' Accademia in Florence. Today, a modern replica of *David* stands in the place where the original once did, outside the Palazzo Vecchio on the Piazza della Signoria in Florence and the original remains in the Accademia.

Taking on Leonardo

Donatello was not the only artist Michelangelo decided

to challenge. At the same time that he was working on *David*, Michelangelo produced a series of marble depictions of the Virgin Mary and the Christ Child in response to Leonardo da Vinci, who was then still the most popular artist in Florence, famous for his Madonna paintings. These included two circular marble *tondi* (plural of *tondo*, which is Latin for *round*) on the theme of the Madonna and Child, the *Pitti Tondo* (1503–5) and the *Taddei Tondo* (1503–5), and one free-standing Madonna, the *Bruges Madonna* (1503–6). The *Bruges Madonna* was commissioned by a Flemish cloth merchant in Bruges, Belgium (hence the name). Contrary to Florentine tradition, Michelangelo did not place the young Jesus on the Virgin Mary's knees but instead depicted a smiling, somewhat chubby child standing between his mother's knees, surrounded by the drapery of her clothing.

At the same time, Michelangelo finished his only authentic panel painting, *The Holy Family*, also known as the *Doni Madonna* (see page 47), painted on a circular canvas, which was often associated with marriage in Renaissance art. The composition of *The Holy Family* is thought to have been inspired by Leonardo da Vinci's lost *cartoon* (i.e., his full-scale drawing for a fresco or

(see page 47)

BACKTRACK:
DONATELLO (1386–1466)

Donatello was one of the greatest sculptors of all time. His bronze statue *David* (c. 1440), now at the Museo Nazionale del Bargello in Florence, was the first free-standing nude statue created since classical antiquity. He devised the technique of the *bas relief* (i.e., shallow relief), a carving done on a very shallow plane, which gave the impression of great depth. He was also the first Renaissance artist to use bronze as a material for sculpture. His other key works include *Judith and Holofernes* (c. 1456–60), a bronze statue at the Palazzo Vecchio in Padua; *Gattamelata* (1447–53), a bronze equestrian statue at the Piazza del Santo in Padua; and *Madonna Pazzi* (c. 1427), a marble relief at the Staätliche Museum in Berlin.

ABOVE

Taddei Tondo. c. 1503–05
Bas relief in marble
Diameter 44.4 x 42.4 x 43.5"
(109 x 104 x 106.5 cm)
Royal Academy of Arts, London

RIGHT

Pitti Tondo (aka *Pitti Madonna*
or *Madonna and Child with
the Infant St. John*)
c. 1503–05. Marble. 33 ³/₈ x 32 ¹/₂"
(84.7 x 82.5 cm)
Museo Nazionale del Bargello, Florence

Bruges Madonna
(aka *Madonna
with Baby*)
1503–6
Marble
Height 48"
(121.9 cm)

BACKTRACK:
**LEONARDO DA VINCI
(1452–1519)**

Leonardo was the quintessential "Renaissance man." In addition to being one of the greatest painters in Italy, he was also a scientist, inventor, and engineer who studied geology, astronomy, botany, optics, and anatomy. It is less well know that Leonardo was also a sculptor. The completion of his most ambitious project, a 24'-high equestrian statue of his patron, Duke Sforza of Milan, was halted after French soldiers used the artist's gigantic clay model of the horse for target practice during their occupation of Milan. Leonardo's key works include *The Last Supper* (1495–97), his magnificent fresco at the Santa Maria delle Grazie in Milan, and the *Mona Lisa* (1503), a painting at the Louvre in Paris.

painting) for the *Madonna and St. Anne*, which Michelangelo had seen in Florence in 1501. It depicts the Virgin as a heroic figure (she was almost certainly painted from a male model) raising her child onto her shoulders with her strong, muscular arms. Commissioned on the occasion of the marriage of **Agnolo Doni** to **Maddalena Strozzi**, of the prominent and wealthy Strozzi Florentine family—the most powerful family in Florence next to the Medici, and rival factions of the latter in the city council—the *Tondo* was Michelangelo's first opportunity to demonstrate his ability as a painter (aside from the full-scale drawing for an unrealized fresco depicting the *Battle of Cascina*, which was supposed to have been painted opposite Leonardo's *Battle of Anghiara* at the Palazzo Vecchio in Florence).

Nightmare on Alms Street: Pope Julius II

When Pope Pius III died in 1503, only ten days after his coronation, Cardinal Giuliano della Rovere (1443–1513) was elected supreme pontiff and took the name **Pope Julius II**. He was 60 years old, had three daughters, and suffered from syphilis. A wealthy man, he commissioned during his rule some of the most important art projects

The Holy Family (aka *Doni Madonna* or *Doni Tondo*) 1503–4. Tempera and oil on panel. Diameter 47 ¹/₄" (120 cm)

Uffizi Gallery, Florence

of the High Renaissance, including the reconstruction of the Basilica of St. Peter's—which Michelangelo would later revise completely—by Italy's foremost architect at the time, **Donato Bramante** (c. 1444–1514), and the decoration of his papal apartments in the Vatican by the painter **Raphael** (1483–1520).

Sound Byte:

"Michelangelo liberated me. In teaching me, by observation, rules that were diametrically opposed to the ones I had been taught, he set me free."
—AUGUSTE RODIN, French sculptor, 1906

Pope Julius II **acquired a dubious reputation for having gained office through bribery and political manipulation.** Prior to his election, he had promised radical political reforms, which included transforming the papacy into a constitutional monarchy governed by the cardinals, and implementing a new rule that would require a two-thirds majority for the papacy to go to war. He not only broke each of his election promises, but he was also notoriously autocratic. Known as the "warrior pope," he personally led the papal forces into war twice during his rule: in 1506 against Perugia and Bologna, and in 1511–12 against the French army. He liked to ride out with his troops in full armor, and dreamed of reviving the medieval Crusade to free Constantinople and

Jerusalem of infidels. His acts of diplomacy and warfare ultimately ensured the return to papal powers of the long-lost Venetian territories. Both the pope's war campaigns and his erratic payments pretty much dictated the progress of Michelangelo's papal projects.

Julius's relationship with Michelangelo was not a match made in heaven but appears to have been one of mutual dependency. The ill-tempered, belligerent pope clearly became the artist's lifelong sparring partner and alter ego—not to mention a great source of income.

In January 1505, the pope called Michelangelo to Rome to create a magnificent tomb that would glorify his memory. Michelangelo had little passion for the commission, however. He did not wish to become stranded on a project that might go on for years, yet he felt unable to resist the pope's request, given the pope's power and financial support.

Michelangelo spent eight months at the quarries in Carrara selecting the marble for the project. When the marble was finally delivered, it filled up half of St. Peter's Square, a spectacle that amazed the citizens of Rome. But by that time, the pope had changed his mind, and during Holy Week of 1506, he closed down all work on his tomb. Michelangelo objected, but Julius, unwilling to discuss the matter further, refused to listen to his protests. In fury, Michelangelo left Rome for Florence.

The painter Raffaello Sanzio, known as Raphael, worked in Florence and later in Rome. Apart from Leonardo da Vinci, he was the only artist who challenged Michelangelo's dominance as the greatest painter of the Renaissance, especially in his ability to create natural beauty. Eight years younger than Michelangelo, Raphael believed in the possibility of a synthesis of the ancient philosophies and Christian theology in art. Among Raphael's key works were his paintings *Madonna with a Goldfinch* (1505–6), at the Uffizi in Florence, and *Pope Julius II* (1511–12), at the National Gallery in London. His fresco *The School of Athens* (1509–11) graces a wall at the Vatican in Rome.

> **FYI: Popes galore**—Remarkably, Michelangelo would be active throughout the reign of 11 popes. Here they are (in chronological order): Pope Alexander VI (1492–1503); Pius III (1503); Julius II (1503–13); Leo X (1513–21); Adrian VI (1521–23); Clement VII (1523–34); Paul III (1534–49); Julius III (1550–55); Marcellus II (1555); Paul IV (1555–59); and Pius IV (1559–65).

In 1506, Pope Julius II, who was then in Bologna, sent for Michelangelo to join him there to produce a 10'-high bronze statue of himself that was to be placed in front of the church of San Petronia as a symbol of his power over the citizens of Bologna. It was during this year that the *Laocoön* group, a Greek sculpture of the Roman period dating from c. 150 B.C., was discovered in Rome. Michelangelo was present at its discovery and was strongly influenced by the work.

After several months of wrangling, Michelangelo agreed to the pope's assignment, mostly because he did not want to create political tension between Rome (i.e., the pope) and Florence. After Michelangelo had grudgingly completed the statue of Julius II, it was accidentally destroyed in the furnace during casting and had to

Laocoön group
c. 150 B.C.

be remade. Ironically, only three years later, during a time of war, the statue was melted down and recast as a cannon. It was sarcastically christened *La Giulia*, undoubtedly alluding to the unpopular pope's fondness for war.

OPPOSITE
Sistine Chapel
with *The Last Judgment* on
the far wall,
above the altar

Hitting the Ceiling: Sistine Chapel (1508–12)

By 1508, another major project was thrust upon Michelangelo by the pope. The sculptor was summoned back to Rome to take over the painting of the ceiling in the Sistine Chapel in the Vatican. Michelangelo felt ill-suited to the job, since he considered himself more a sculptor than a painter, and was certainly not a *fresco* painter (*fresco* is a painting on plaster that is still wet, or "fresh," and that dries with the plaster). But Julius insisted, and on May 10, 1508, the 33-year-old sculptor began work on the ceiling.

The Sistine Chapel had been built between 1477 and 1484 by Pope Sixtus IV. It was designed according to the proportions of Solomon's Temple in Jerusalem: The chapel is approximately 132' long x 67' high x 44' wide. Created for private religious functions at the papal court, it can be accessed directly from the pope's residential quarters. During the early 1480s, the walls had been decorated by the principal Italian painters of the time, including Botticelli, Ghirlandaio, and **Pietro Vanucci Perugino** (c. 1472–1523). The original ceiling had been painted blue with golden stars.

The original plan for the ceiling called for Michelangelo to paint only those areas between the arches now occupied by the prophets and sibyls (i.e., prophetesses of classical antiquity who, according to medieval belief, predicted the birth of Christ). Michelangelo persuaded the pope that something grander was needed. The final design most likely resulted from negotiations among the pope, the artist, and a team of theological advisors. Although Michelangelo had apprenticed under the Ghirlandaios for the decoration of the Tornabuoni Chapel in St. Maria Novella in Florence in 1488, this was his first fully executed fresco.

It took Michelangelo four years to complete the project. During this time, he painted more than 350 larger-than-life figures, on a vault surface that covered 5,000 square feet (larger than a tennis court). The work began with elaborate *cartoons* (i.e., drawings on paper) of most of the figures on the ceiling. Before the

Sistine Ceiling
Fresco on one end of the ceiling of the Sistine Chapel
1508–12

actual painting was begun, the ceiling surfaces were prepared by applying a coat of rough plaster, the *arriccio*, and then by laying over this a final smooth coat, the *intonaco*, on which Michelangelo and his assistants would paint.

The outlines of the figures were transposed by dusting powdered charcoal or colored chalk through holes punctured into the cartoons or by engraving the wet plaster with a scalpel or stylus.

The central-vault area features nine scenes from the Book of Genesis, divided into three groups: The first depicts God's creation of the universe; the second, the story of Adam and Eve and their expulsion from paradise; and the third, the sacrifice of Noah and the flood. These central scenes are surrounded by images of prophets and sibyls. Other Old Testament subjects, including the ancestors of Christ, are depicted in the lunettes and the overhanging *spandrels* (i.e., the

Sistine Ceiling
Fresco on the other end of the ceiling of the Sistine Chapel. 1508–12

ABOVE
Studies for the *Libyan Sibyl*
c. 1511. Red chalk on paper
11 ³/₈ x 8 ³/₈"
(27.93 x 20.58 cm)

RIGHT
Libyan Sibyl, fresco in the
Sistine Chapel. 1511–12

areas between the arches just below the images of the prophets and sibyls).

> **FYI:** Michelangelo used male models for the female figures in the Sistine Chapel. A good example of this practice is the drawing for the *Libyan Sibyl* in the collection of The Metropolitan Museum of Art in New York. The gender transformation was achieved during the painting process by softening the contours of the figures, but the resulting women appear mannish despite the alterations.

Contrary to legend, Michelangelo did not work alone, nor did he paint lying on his back. His team of contractors included plasterers, painting assistants, apprentices, color grinders, and handymen. Like all artists of his time, he employed assistants and apprentices who would make the first rough cuts into the marble, or paint the backgrounds and decorative elements of his frescoes. The chapel had to remain in use by the cardinals and the papal court during the entire time, and no paint or plaster was allowed to drop onto the chapel floors. The work was made more difficult because the vault was curved. Michelangelo devised a special scaffolding that rose 50 feet above the pavement below. It was essentially a movable platform with steps on either side, supported by wooden beams.

Marcello Venusti
Portrait of Michelangelo at the time of the Sistine Chapel. c. 1535

The ceiling was painted in three stages. The first stage ended when, during the winter of 1508–9, a fierce wind caused salt and (later) mold to appear in several places. The second stage ended halfway through the project when the pope left Rome for almost a year, leaving Michelangelo with no funds or instructions. The final stage was completed on October 31, 1512.

Michelangelo employed a variety of paints and techniques. His innovative use of thin, almost translucent, watercolorlike paint resulted in extraordinarily luminous and iridescent surfaces, most strikingly apparent in the skin of the snake in the Garden of Eden.

Unlike the central scenes, the lunettes above the windows were painted rapidly (one each day) without the guide-

LEFT
Study for *The Creation of Adam*
Sistine Ceiling. Red chalk drawing

BELOW
The Creation of Adam, fresco on the
ceiling, Sistine Chapel. 1508–12
Vatican, Rome

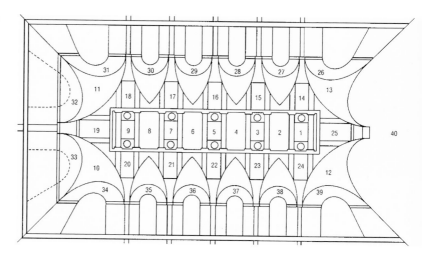

lines of cartoons. They are less refined but show greater expressive freedom. The finished ceiling was shown to the public for the first time in October 1512, and the pope died four months later at the age of 70.

The Sistine ceiling is the major work of Michelangelo's career. It established him as the leading painter of his time. The extraordinary feat of his having undertaken a project on this scale, with little previous experience in fresco painting, and executed under less than favorable working conditions, forced him to create new techniques and stylistic innovations. It is, to this day, the most spectacular confluence of architecture and painting. Never before had anyone produced such visual unity of architecture and art, or fused the principles of painting and sculpture so effortlessly.

Throughout the centuries, the ceiling of the Sistine Chapel grew grimy and dirty, in part because of the smoke from years of candle-burning. In 1980, a major cleaning and restoration of the ceiling of the Sistine Chapel was undertaken. It took nine years to complete.

The areas painted in fresco were treated with AB-57, a mixture of ammonium bicarbonate, sodium bicarbonate, an antifungicide, and a cellulose-based substance that was allowed to stay on the area being cleaned for about three minutes and then removed with a natural sponge soaked in twice-distilled water. The so-called water-soluble *a secco* parts (i.e., those that are painted after the plaster has dried) were cleaned with organic solvents.

More than 15,000 photographs were shot before, during, and after the restoration, including images taken with infrared and ultraviolet light. Photo data were stored on computers. In addition, the process was recorded by Tokyo-based Nippon Television Network (NTA) on some 45,000 meters of 16mm film.

Sound Byte:
> *"A man paints with his brains and not with his hands."*
> —MICHELANGELO

Back to the Tomb of Julius II

Even though Julius II was dead, the issue of his tomb was far from resolved. In 1513, the pope's estate contracted with the 38-year-old Michelangelo to begin work on the tomb once again. For the next 30 years, the artist would obsess over the project. He produced at least six different designs and a number of marble carvings, including the so-called *Slaves*, that were ultimately discarded. After continued interruptions caused by commissions from other popes, he completed the *Tomb of Julius II* in 1545. Forty years after it had begun, the "tragedy of the tomb," as Michelangelo's friend and biographer Ascanio Condivi referred to it, finally came to an end.

The central figure in the final version of the *Tomb* is the overpowering statue of a giant seated *Moses*. Included in Michelangelo's original design for the tomb and carved during the years 1513 to 1515, it possesses the technical virtuosity of his earlier sculptures. The bearded face, with its penetrating gaze, is considered by many to be a self-portrait of Michelangelo as well as a depiction of the late and detested pope.

National Gallery, London

ABOVE
Raphael
Pope Julius II. c. 1511–12
Oil on panel. 44 x 33"
(108 x 80.7 cm)

OPPOSITE
Tomb of Pope Julius II
1505–45. Marble. Height
103 ¹/₂ x 61 ¹/₂"
(263 x 156 cm)

Moses
1513–15
Marble
Height 7'7"
(235 cm)
Tomb of Pope
Julius II

Why the Horns?

Instead of endowing Moses with a radiating halo from his head, as described in the Old Testament, Michelangelo sculpted him with two horns on the top of his head—the result of a mistranslation of the Hebrew word for "light" into Latin. The first translation of the Bible from the Hebrew into Latin—known as the "Vulgate Bible"—was made in the year 405 by Saint Jerome (c. 347–c. 420). Saint Jerome was one of the Latin Fathers and a hermit. The Bible says that when Moses descended from Mount Sinai with a second set of the Ten Commandments, after the Golden Calf had been destroyed, his head was adorned with rays of light. Jerome mistranslated the Hebrew word for light and thought it said "horns," which resulted in a description of Moses' head adorned with horns.

Michelangelo carved six figures representing slaves (also called "captives") for the tomb of Pope Julius II. Two of them, the so-called *Dying Slave* and *Rebellious Slave*, were made between 1513 and 1516. Four others, the *Accademia Slaves*—which include *The Young Slave, Awakening Slave,* and *Atlas Slave* (shown on page 69)—were carved between 1519 and 1534. (The fourth, *Bearded Slave*, is not shown here.) None of the *Slaves*, however, was incorporated into the completed tomb.

How two *Slaves* ended up in Paris

Between the years 1544 and 1546, Michelangelo became ill and moved

RIGHT
Dying Slave
from the Tomb
of Pope Julius II
Marble statue
1513–15
Height 7' 6 ½"
(222 cm)

OPPOSITE
LEFT TO RIGHT
Young Slave
1519–34
Marble
Height 8' 6 ¾"
(252 cm)

*Awakening
Slave*
1519–34
Marble
Height 9'
(265 cm)

Atlas Slave
1519–34
Marble
Height 9' 1 ½"
(268.3 cm)

into an apartment at the palace of the Roman banker Roberto Strozzi. Upon his recovery, he thanked Strozzi for the care he had received in his house by presenting him with the two earlier *Slaves*. However, soon after receiving this extraordinary gift, Strozzi gave the *Slaves* to the King of France, **Francis I**. After Francis I died in 1547, his son, **Henry III**, unloaded the sculptures onto Henri Duc de Montmorency, who installed them in the courtyard of his château. After Montmorency's son was executed in 1632 for taking part in a conspiracy against Cardinal Richelieu, his belongings—included Michelangelo's *Slaves*—were confiscated and placed in Richelieu's art collection at his château in Poitou, France. Later, Richelieu had the *Slaves* brought to his Parisian townhouse, the locale of his many amorous affairs. During the French Revolution, the *Slaves* were seized, and in 1794 they were placed in the collection of the Louvre in Paris, where they remain to this day. The four later *Slaves* are now, like Michelangelo's *David*, on view at the Galleria dell'Accademia in Florence.

The Fiasco of San Lorenzo

In 1515, Michelangelo was hard at work on the tomb for Julius II when the new pope, **Leo X** (1475–1521), a Medici, asked him to decorate the bare façade of San Lorenzo, the Medici family church in Florence. Though he tried for three years to develop a plan, the sculptor was able to produce only drawings, a wooden model of the façade (see opposite page, top), and wax figures. Excessive redesigns, production delays, and political complications eventually led to the cancellation of the project by the pope, in spite of the vast sums of money that had been poured into it. The façade, which Michelangelo had predicted would become "a mirror of architecture and of sculpture to all Italy," had turned into one of Florence's biggest architectural flops. During the three years of Michelangelo's supervision of the project, no actual work was done on the façade. To this day, it remains the same as it was in Michelangelo's time: a blank brick wall.

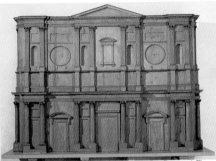

LEFT
Wooden model for the façade of the
Medici Chapel, San Lorenzo, Florence

BELOW
San Lorenzo, Florence, with the
Medici Chapel (small dome at far right)

A Scare from the North

In 1521, shortly after Michelangelo began work on the Medici Chapel, Pope Leo X died, and a new pope, **Adrian VI** (1459–1523), the Dutch Cardinal Adrian of Utrecht, was elected to succeed him. Adrian VI was an ardent reformer of the Church, with no interest in spending money on the arts. Outraged by the nudity of Michelangelo's frescoes on the Sistine Chapel ceiling, he threatened to have them overpainted. Fortunately for Western civilization (and Italian tourism), Adrian VI died only two years after becoming pope, and the next pontiff, **Clement VII** (1478–1534), was again a member of the Medici family.

A Time of War

Italy during the early 1500s was scarred by territorial struggles between **King Francis I** (1494–1547) of France and **Charles V** (1500–1558), the Holy Roman Emperor. To protect its own interests, the papacy switched alliances frequently. In May 1527, a large army of Italian, Spanish, and German troops, many of them Lutherans led by the emperor, entered Rome, murdering citizens, plundering buildings, and desecrating religious sites. In December, Pope Clement VII fled to Orvieto. In the fallout from these events, the Medici lost power and were exiled from the city of Florence, which was again declared a republic.

In 1529, the pope reconciled with the emperor, and Florence began to prepare for war against the imperial and papal forces who wanted to restore power to the Medici. Michelangelo was appointed to Florence's military council and put in charge of reinforcing existing bastions and designing fortifications for the city. He even traveled to Ferrara to study the military architecture there. Only a few drawings documenting these activities remain. None of Michelangelo's military designs were ever built.

Living Dangerously

After a 10-month siege of the city by imperial troops and a coup d'état within the Florentine government, the Medici family regained control of the city. During a full-scale act of reprisal against the enemies of the Medici, the new temporary governor of Florence ordered that Michelangelo be assassinated. Fortunately, Michelangelo was quickly pardoned by the pope, who wanted him to continue his work on the Medici Chapel.

The Accidental Minimalist

Renaissance architecture was characterized by its emphasis on public space. Until then, architecture's primary character was regarded that of enclosing space (with paintings representing space, and sculpture displacing space). As we see in Michelangelo's painting of the Sistine Chapel ceiling and his design for the Medici chapel, these rigid divisions

Domed ceiling of the
New Sacristy of the
Medici Chapel
San Lorenzo, Florence
1520–34

among architecture, painting, and sculpture became more fluid during the High Renaissance.

During the Renaissance, architecture was not considered a specialized profession and was practiced by painters and sculptors, among them, Michelangelo, Leonardo da Vinci, and Giorgio Vasari. The three foremost professional architects were **Filippo Brunelleschi** (1377–1466), **Donato Bramante** (1444–1514), and **Leon Battista Alberti** (1404–1472). Brunelleschi's most famous design is that for the cupola of the Florence cathedral. It was the first building since classical antiquity to having been designed with the outside of the building in mind rather than the inside.

In September 1519, despite the fiasco of the façade, Michelangelo was commissioned by the pope to design a memorial chapel with an adjacent library—the Laurentian Library—for the Medici family at San Lorenzo and to carve several funerary statues for the chapel.

As was the case with so many of Michelangelo's projects, the library was begun reluctantly by the artist and was never completed, mostly due to cutbacks of papal funds and to the political unrest in Florence. This was Michelangelo's first major architectural commission

Interior of the Medici Chapel
San Lorenzo, Florence, with
(on the left wall) *Tomb of
Giuliano de' Medici* and
(centered on the wall above)
Madonna and Child

and it became, unintentionally, his most minimalist work. In addition to designing the architecture, Michelangelo carved a total of seven figures for the chapel: *Madonna and Child,* four allegories (*Dawn, Dusk, Night,* and *Day*), and the statues of Lorenzo and Giuliano de' Medici.

Michelangelo conceived the tombs of Giuliano and Lorenzo to face each other on separate walls, with each sarcophagus holding two allegorical figures and the *Madonna and Child* placed in front of a third wall. It is one of Michelangelo's most impressive carvings and forms the spiritual center of the composition. The relationship of the Madonna to the two tombs and the integration of the sculpture into the architecture form a visual unity never before accomplished in a funerary chapel.

If you stand facing the wall that houses the *Madonna and Child,* you will see, on the wall to the right, the Tomb of Lorenzo de' Medici, and, on the left, the tomb of Giuliano de' Medici. The austere, elegant beauty of the Medici Chapel, as it is experienced today, is evoked in part by its incompleteness (the spare furnishing of sculptures and the absence of any wall painting) and in part by the contrast among the serene blue-gray sandstone (*pietra serena*), the shiny white marble of the sculptures and doorways, and the bare whitewashed walls.

Tomb of Lorenzo de' Medici, with figures of *Dusk* (left) and *Dawn* (right) below *Lorenzo*. 1526–34 Marble

The figure of
Night on the
Tomb of Giuliano
de' Medici. 1521–34
Marble

The figure of *Day*
on the Tomb of
Giuliano
de' Medici
1521–34. Marble

Booking another Job: Laurentian Library

The Laurentian Library is located above the cells for the monks in the monastery of San Lorenzo, adjacent to the chapel. An outlandish, triple-sectioned staircase in the lobby leads to the reading room, which is about ten feet above the floor level of the monastic cells. Its innovative form has been likened to a flow of lava. The central stairs were reserved for the Medici ruler, while the side stairs were to be used by his entourage. Today it is a prime example of early Mannerist architecture.

FYI: The reading room of the Laurentian Library features rows of wooden reading desks. Unlike today's libraries, it has no bookshelves, since the manuscripts, in the time of Michelangelo, were stored on the desks themselves.

Bacchus revisited

In 1530, Michelangelo carved a small and delicate statue of *Apollo* for the governor of Florence. It was reportedly executed in record time and it, too, was left incomplete. *Apollo* was one of the first serpentine figures (i.e., his body gives the effect of a continuous spiral motion). Unlike the earlier *Bacchus*, *Apollo* is not missing any vital body parts.

OPPOSITE
Stairway to the reading room of the Laurentian Library
c. 1521–34

BELOW
Apollo. c. 1530
Marble
Height 57 ½"
(146 cm)
with base

Bargello, Florence

Painter of "Obscenities": *The Last Judgment* (1536–41)

In 1533, Pope Clement VII wrote to Michelangelo, asking him return to Rome to begin work on an exciting new project: to paint the resurrection of Christ on the altar wall of the Sistine Chapel at the Vatican, since the wall had been damaged by fire in 1525. Two days after Michelangelo arrived in Rome, however, Clement VII died. He was succeeded by **Pope Paul III** (1468–1549), a longtime admirer of Michelangelo, who promptly appointed him to the salaried and highly prestigious post of Supreme Architect, Painter, and Sculptor to the Vatican household.

When Michelangelo's contract was renewed by the new pope in 1535, the subject chosen was no longer that of the Risen Christ but of the Last Judgment.

It turned out to be the largest fresco ever painted, measuring 45 x 40'. At the apex of the ascending movement within the vast composition stands a beardless Christ as judge, flanked by St. John the Baptist on his left, and by the Virgin Mary on his right, and accompanied by Herculean male angels. Christ's right hand is raised in a gesture of damnation, while his left hand is extended gently as if to summon the blessed to heaven.

BACKTRACK:
MANNERISM (1520–1600)

Mannerism, a movement in art and architecture that became popular in Italy around 1520, broke with the classicism of the High Renaissance and was known for its elongated, contorted figures, crowded compositions, confused scale and spatial relationships, and a flattening of the picture plane. In architecture, it was expressed in unbalanced proportions and arbitrary arrangements of decoration. Named after the term *maniera*, used by the art historian Giorgio Vasari when he described the Late Renaissance style of art, Mannerism officially began in Rome with Raphael's *Fire of Borgo* frescoes and in Florence with Michelangelo's design of the Laurentian Library. Other artists who worked in the Mannerist style were **Jacopo Carucci da Pontormo** (1494–1557), **Rosso Fiorintino** (c. 1495–1540), and **Parmigianino** (1503–1540).

Michelangelo did not paint wings or halos. He preferred to concentrate on the human body. His women are usually clothed, while men are painted in the nude (with the exception of Christ, whose private parts are covered a loincloth). In the Middle Ages and Renaissance, unlike today, the female body was generally considered to be aesthetically inferior to the male's, in accordance with the biblical account that Adam was created in the image of God, whereas Eve was "only" a second-generation copy (hence Michelangelo's preference for using male models for his female figure studies).

PREVIOUS SPREAD
The Last Judgment
fresco in the Sistine Chapel
1536–41
45 x 40'
(13.7 x 12.2 m)
Located at the end wall, at the chapel altar

Michelangelo's depiction of the angels as nude beings was particularly provocative. Whereas earlier artists had painted the damned in hell as naked beings, they always portrayed angels in heaven fully clothed. Michelangelo dared to dissolve the traditional hierarchy between heaven and hell by depicting all figures as equal parts of a large community of fate.

> **FYI:** Below Christ's left foot in *The Last Judgment*, St. Bartholomew is depicted holding his flayed (i.e., stripped off) skin onto which Michelangelo painted his self-portrait. Look on page 82, slightly to the right of the center of the fresco, and you'll see his face painted on the dangling skin.

To accommodate the enormous painting, Michelangelo had to destroy two of the lunettes that he had earlier painted as part of the Sistine Chapel ceiling. Perugino's frescoed altarpiece of the Assumption was

Virgin Mary and Christ
Detail from *The Last Judgment* fresco in the Sistine Chapel 1536–41

also demolished in the process, and the two original windows were filled in with bricks to become part of the painting.

The Last Judgment, his first painting since the Sistine Chapel ceiling, is executed in Michelangelo's later style. The figures are broader and fuller, with heavier proportions. To accommodate the fresco's immense size, Michelangelo applied striking increases in scale as the figures ascend.

(A footnote: After Michelangelo's death, Pope Pius V ordered most of the nudity in *The Last Judgment* to be painted over as *breeches* (i.e., painted loincloths). More clothing was added in the next three centuries. Most of the breeches were removed during the recent restoration of *The Last Judgment* that followed the cleaning of the Sistine ceiling.)

FYI: Michelangelo delighted in taking revenge on his harshest critics. In *The Last Judgment*, he represented the Papal Master of Ceremonies, Biagi da Cesena—who had complained to the pope about the display of genitalia in Michelangelo's frescoes—as Minos, the pagan Judge of the Underworld, his naked, bulging body enwrapped by a snake biting his genitals. When Biagi protested to the pope about the insult, the pope wisely replied that he had no power to release people from Hell, only from Purgatory. To add injury to insult, Michelangelo placed Biagi's portrait at the lower-right corner of the altar wall, near the door through which Biagi would have to enter and exit the chapel. (See opposite page.) The pope was amused.

*Minos, the pagan
Judge of the
Underworld*
Detail from
*The Last
Judgment*
fresco in the
Sistine Chapel
1536–41

Vatican, Rome

The Last Judgment
Detail of the
fresco in the
Sistine Chapel
1536–41

When *The Last Judgment* was revealed in 1541, Pope Paul III was said to have dropped to his knees in prayer. However, Michelangelo's painting was not universally admired. The Florentine art critic **Pietro Aretino** (1492–1556) declared the painting to be better suited for a "voluptuous bath-house."

Sculptor as poet

Michelangelo began writing verses while living in the Medici palace. Whenever he could not express himself through his sculpture or painting, he turned to poetry. While he was certainly no more than an amateur writer, his verses have attracted the interest of some of the greatest poets of all time. From Wordsworth to Rilke, poets have struggled with translating Michelangelo's poems into their respective languages. After Michelangelo met (and fell in love with) the Roman aristocrat **Tommaso de' Cavalieri** in 1532, his literary output almost quadrupled. His passion for Cavalieri and, later, for the poet **Vittoria Colonna** (see page 108), inspired him to write hundreds of sonnets and madrigals (an Italian lyrical form consisting of 6 to 15 verses), in addition to his regular correspondence. In his poems to Cavalieri, Michelangelo praises his lover's beauty but also stresses the innocence of his affection, probably to avoid any scandals. There are also many references to the artist's advanced age (he was in his 50s when he met the 23-year-old Cavalieri) and to his own diminishing physical attraction.

Michelangelo's friendship with the Florentine nobleman and humanist **Luigi del Riccio**, whom he met around the time he began *The Last Judgment*, became instrumental to the artist's poetic production in his later years. At the artist's request, del Riccio, who worked as a banker in Rome and had won Michelangelo's trust over the years, edited the artist's verses for a planned publication of Michelangelo's poems. (The planned edition of Michelangelo's poems was later abandoned, when del Riccio died unexpectedly in the summer of 1546. A first edition of his poems was not published until long after the artist's death, in 1623, by one of his grandnephews.)

Keeping the Popes at Bay

While Michelangelo regularly complained about being a slave to the papacy, he quickly learned how to keep the popes off his neck. His relationships with them were clearly love-hate affairs. One could not survive without the other, but they often made each other's lives as difficult as possible.

In his later years, Michelangelo was not shy about putting the pope firmly in his place. Upon accepting the position of chief architect for the reconstruction of St. Peter's in Rome in 1540, he demanded unprecedented artistic autonomy. When, during the course of the project, Cardinal Cervini complained to Michelangelo that he had not first cleared certain design changes with him, the artist replied, "Your duty is to collect the money and guard it against thieves and you must leave the task of designing the building to me." Michelangelo then turned to the pope, reminding him that he was doing this work without pay (he did it for his "spiritual satisfaction"), and that unless he could do it his way, it would be a waste of his time.

While Michelangelo derived his main source of income and fame from the papacy, he routinely solicited and accepted commissions from other wealthy clients, such as the King of France, even though he knew that these commissions would clash with the deadlines for his papal commissions. He was so eager to carve and paint for the French court that he promised to keep working in heaven, should he die prematurely.

The Last Paintings

During the final years of working on the tomb for Julius II, Michelangelo also painted two large frescoes for the Vatican chapel of Pope Paul II: *Conversion of St. Paul* (1542–46) and *Crucifixion of St. Peter* (1545–50). (See following spread for paintings.)

Less well known than the frescoes of the Sistine Chapel, these are two of Michelangelo's most expressive works, painted in his late, Mannerist style. The flattened picture plane and the off-centered axis in the *Conversion of St. Paul*, and the diagonal composition in the *Crucifixion of St. Peter*, are Mannerist devices. The artist also completely abandoned the Renaissance perspective, reverting to the medieval painting style:

OVERLEAF
LEFT
Conversion of St. Paul (Saul)
1542–46. Fresco
Pauline Chapel

RIGHT
Crucifixion of St. Peter
1545–50. Fresco
Pauline Chapel

What is *behind* is, instead, represented *above*. The diagonal composition was required by the orientation of St. Peter's cross, which was inspired by St. Peter's request to be crucified upside down as a show of reverence for the crucifixion of Christ. In a startling gesture, St. Peter turns his head outward, his piercing eyes fixated on the viewer.

In another twist on Michelangelo's biased representation of gender, male and female figures are painted here without real distinction, so that, in many instances, gender identification is virtually impossible. Even the women's breasts resemble little more than male pectoral muscles.

The frescoes featuring St. Paul (aka the "Paulinian" frescoes) were painted by an aging Michelangelo who suffered from kidney stones and who described himself in one of his poems as a "bogeyman" dressed in rags and plagued by illnesses. His later style was characterized by rough, unpolished surfaces, an incomplete rendering of forms, and expressive articulation.

Michelangelo the Architect

Michelangelo approached architecture, as he did painting, with the hand, eye, and mind of a sculptor. Amazingly, Michelangelo's most intensive period of architecture did not begin until he was 71 years old.

In 1540, Michelangelo was appointed chief architect in charge of the reconstruction of the Basilica of St. Peter's in Rome, replacing the

The drum, dome,
and lantern of
St. Peter's, Rome
1546–64

Wooden model for the cupola of St. Peter's, Rome. 1558–61

architect **Angelo da Sangallo**, who had died in 1534. Unquestionably the most prestigious architectural commission of its time, the commission meant more to Michelangelo than money and fame. It became, in his words, a matter of "spiritual satisfaction."

The Sangallo Gang

For 40 years, the reconstruction of St. Peter's had been essentially stalled, bogged down by corruption, lack of money, shoddy construction, and an erratic labor force. Michelangelo wasn't subtle in his disdain for Sangallo's design. When Sangallo's followers were showing him Sangallo's model for the basilica for the first time, claiming that it was "a meadow where there is always good grazing," Michelangelo hinted that it might be more suitable as a pasture for sheep or oxen who knew nothing about art. In a letter to the administrators of the basilica, he explained that Sangallo's design lacked sufficient light and that its many columns would create dark niches that would provide shelter to thieves and "nun-rapists."

When the pope asked him to accept the position of chief architect, Michelangelo even publicly challenged

Interior of
the dome of
St. Peter's

Sangallo's followers to do whatever they could to convince the pope not to hire him. Why? Because if he were to accept the job, he would make sure that none of them would continue to be involved in the project.

When it became clear that Michelangelo would abandon Sangallo's existing plans for St. Peter's (and that he even arranged for the demolition of those portions that had already been built), not surprisingly Sangallo's followers (whom Vasari called the "Sangallo Gang") turned against him. Michelangelo's response to the Sangallo Gang's attacks was to refuse to be paid for his work, thus demonstrating his independence from Sangallo's followers and his own incorruptibility. (He also wisely kept his distance from the construction site by overseeing the work from his studio.)

The growing resistance to Michelangelo at St. Peter's finally forced the pope to issue a formal brief, once and for all declaring that Michelangelo's design must be respected.

For the new St. Peter's, Michelangelo conceived a unified, cross-and-square plan for the interior, with a light-filled dome featuring broad ribs that gave an illusion of height. Michelangelo directed the project for 17 years but, tragically, would not live to see it completed.

Mapping Rome

Through his various architectural projects, Michelangelo became the leading urban planner of 16th-century Rome. In 1538, Pope Paul II asked him to design the Campidoglio, an area on top of the Capitoline Hill in Rome that had been little more than an uneven ground of beaten earth. Michelangelo created a square framed by three symmetrical buildings, decorated with an intricate oval inset with a star-shaped pattern that symbolized the world in the tradition of ancient floor mosaics. It played an important role in the history of urban planning and remains one of the most elegant urban squares in Europe.

The artist's last urban project was the Porta Pia. The then-existing system of ancient Roman roads was no longer capable of handling the growing traffic of pilgrims to the Holy City. New roads were developed, which necessitated the construction of new gates at the city wall. The most spectacular boulevard was the Via Pia, named after Pope Pius IV (it is now called Via Venti Settembre). Its gateway was designed by Michelangelo between 1561 and 1564. His major innovation consisted

The Campidoglio
Rome

ABOVE
Study for the Porta Pia
1561. Black chalk, pen and
brown ink, wash
and white heightening
17 ⅛ x 11 ⅛"
(43.5 x 28.3 cm)

LEFT
The Porta Pia, Rome
1561–64. (The central
superstructure was
added in 1853.)

of inverting the gate's orientation, facing it inward, toward the city, rather than outward. (In the 19th century, a second story was added to the gate.)

Last Sculptures

While he was busy painting the Paulinian frescoes, Michelangelo began work on another *pietà*, the so-called Florentine *Pietà*, a multi-figure composition that includes, in addition to Mary Magdalene and a lifeless Christ, the figure of Nicodemus gazing down at Christ. Iconographically, the sculpture is a mixture of a Deposition (i.e., Descent from the Cross) and a Lamentation. The execution and emotional content of this sculpture are radically different from those of the earlier *Pietà*. Overwhelming grief, suffering, and resignation are seen in each figure's face, while the heads of Christ and Mary appear fused in a common spirituality. To merge two figures into one was a unique formal conception in the 16th century.

But like so many other works, the Florentine *Pietà* was never completed. Impelled by several flaws in the marble, the artist smashed it to pieces. The remains were given to one of Michelangelo' s servants, who sold it to the collector Francesco Bandini. With Michelangelo's approval, Bandini had parts of Christ's body restored, but in its present form it is still missing the left leg. It is now housed in the museum of the cathedral of Florence, the Museo dell'Opera Duomo.

Castello Sforzesco, Milan

Pietà Rondanini. 1564
Marble. Height 76 ³/₄" (185 cm)

It was not, however, Michelangelo's last *pietà*. He spent the last ten years of his life carving his final sculpture, the *Pietà Rondanini*. The statue, which incorporated fragments of an earlier sculpture, such as a polished unattached arm, would have been considered by many during Michelangelo's time to be no more than a relic. Over the centuries, however, it has achieved the status of one of the world's great sculptures and is acknowledged as the artist's final masterpiece.

The *Pietà Rondanini,* an unfinished work, depicts the figures of Mary and Christ in an enraptured embrace, almost merging into each other, in a way that recalls the Florentine *Pietà*. But this work is endowed with a dramatically intensified spirituality. Both bodies have been deprived of any trace of physical beauty.

Michelangelo carved at least two earlier versions from the stone. Except for those parts that belong to the earlier versions, the marble is roughhewn and unpolished. The artist worked feverishly on the sculpture until the day he died at the age of 89. Unable to sleep, he is said to have worked all night, using a cardboard helmet upon which he attached a candle.

Sound Byte:

"I saw Michelangelo at work. He had passed his sixtieth year, and although he was not very strong, yet in a quarter of an hour he caused more splinters to fall from a very hard block of marble than three young masons in three or four times as long. He attacked the work with such energy and fire that I thought it would fly into pieces."

—BLAISE DE VIGENÈRE, local citizen, 1550

Michelangelo also found time, during his final years, to design a monumental equestrian statue that was to be cast in bronze, not wholly unlike the one that Leonardo da Vinci had attempted many years earlier. It had been commissioned in 1559 by Catherine de' Medici, the widow of King Henry II of France, to commemorate her husband. Due to his advanced age, Michelangelo did not model or cast the sculpture himself but delegated it to his friend Daniele da Volterra. Only the horse was completed and sent to France, where politics again determined its fate. It did not fare much better than Leonardo's clay horse or the bronze of Julius II: In 1793, during the French Revolution, it was melted down.

Michelangelo's "Stone"

OPPOSITE
Design 69 F
anatomical
drawing

Around 1547, the time Michelangelo began to carve the Florentine *Pietà*, he developed a kidney stone—an ironic ailment for someone who dealt in "stone" all his life. He suffered from painful attacks, a lack of sleep, and an inability to urinate. His main treatment consisted of drinking water from the springs of Viterbo. His "stone," as he referred to it, became a detailed subject in many of his letters and poems.

Why were so many of Michelangelo's Sculptures left unfinished?

In fact, most of Michelangelo's sculptures were never completed. While his contemporaries accepted this phenomenon as a signature of the artist's evolving style, some tried to offer more rational theories, as in the case of the bust of *Brutus*. It was never completed, probably due to Michelangelo's overcommitted schedule, which necessitated simultaneous work on the Julius tomb and the two frescoes for the Paulinian Chapel.

While Michelangelo did abandon a number of projects after having agreed to too many commissions, the unfinished (*non finito*) quality of his later sculptures is often the result of conscious stylistic decisions on his part. The *Accademia Slaves* (see page 69) were conceived to signify their captivity by leaving part of their bodies trapped within the marble, straining for release. In his later years, Michelangelo moved away from the idealized beauty of his *David* and *Pietà* toward a more expressive and mannered style. He was reported to have said on his deathbed that his greatest regret was that he was dying just as he was beginning to learn how to be a sculptor.

The Gay issue

By most accounts, Michelangelo was gay. While the sexual practice of sodomy was punishable by death in Florence, the authorities rarely invoked this punishment, perhaps because many prominent Renaissance artists, including Leonardo da Vinci and Benvenuto Cellini, were gay or bisexual.

Michelangelo is believed to have had several male lovers, the most prominent of whom was the young Roman nobleman Tommaso de' Cavalieri, who inspired most of the love sonnets written by the artist. He made a large number of so-called presentation drawings of the young men he desired—drawings in which naked men lie sprawling with their legs wide open—and made gifts of these drawings to his potential lovers. Tommaso and Michelangelo were close for more than 30 years.

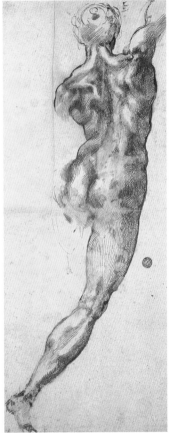

Casa Buonarroti, Florence

Vittoria Colonna. c. 1536
Pen-and-ink drawing over
red chalk with hatching

Men seem to have been the only objects of Michelangelo's amorous affections. But at the age of 61, he met the poet **Vittoria Colonna** (1492–1547), the Marchesa di Pescare, a wealthy widow for whom he would develop a deeply Platonic attachment. (Ironically, he felt that Vittoria had the soul of a man.) Her husband had been killed in battle 11 years earlier and the ardently religious woman spent much of her time living in a convent, where she regularly held a *salon* in which she entertained literary figures, artists, and clergymen. Like Cavalieri, she inspired many of Michelangelo's love poems and some of his most deeply spiritual and accomplished drawings. But the love was almost certainly of a nonsexual nature, even though their correspondence was at times charmingly romantic. Michelangelo once sent Vittoria a gallant note written on blue paper, which said that "of divine things one speaks in a blue field," alluding to the heavenly state of their relationship. Her death in 1547 came as an insufferable blow to Michelangelo, one from which he would never fully recover.

Family Matters

When his older brother became a Dominican monk, Michelangelo assumed the role of the oldest son and the responsibilities that traditionally came with it. Throughout his life, Michelangelo showed concern for his family's financial well-being, health, and safety during the frequent political turmoils of the time.

He regularly sent money to his father and brothers and, later, to his nephew Lionardo. In 1508 he bought three adjacent houses (including the present Casa Buonarroti) for himself and his family. He also owned a farm near Pozzolatico, which he had purchased in 1506 for investment purposes, and his family owned a house and farm in Settignano. When his aunt successfully sued his father for the recovery of her sister's dowry after the death of Michelangelo's mother, he paid her off. Later he helped his brothers set up a wool business, and he even registered himself with the Wool Guild.

Michelangelo could also be ill-tempered: When his nephew Lionardo sent a package to him in Rome, containing a couple of new shirts, he wrote back that he was "amazed" that Lionardo would send him shirts of such bad quality, "since they are so coarse that there is not a single peasant here who wouldn't be ashamed to wear them."

He regularly wrote scolding letters to his brothers and once even threatened to mount his horse and ride all the way from Rome back to Florence to settle things.

Once Michelangelo even exploded in anger at his father, when he learned that he had drawn money from Michelangelo's bank account without first asking his son's permission.

Sound Byte:

"They say that if you treat a good man kindly you make him even better, and if you treat a wicked man so you make him worse. I've tried now for many years with kind words and deeds to lead you back to a decent way of life at peace with your father and the rest of us, and yet you grow worse all the time. I am not telling you that you are wicked, but in the way you carry on you will never ever please me, or the others."

—MICHELANGELO, to his younger brother Giovansimone, 1509

Detail of *Young Archer*
(aka *Cupid*)

A Cupid in New York?

Just prior to carving the *Pietà*, Michelangelo made a *Cupid* or *Apollo* for his Roman patron Jacopo Galli. A statue that was attributed to the school of Michelangelo appeared at auction in London in 1902, but apparently did not sell and subsequently disappeared from public record. In 1996, a leading Renaissance scholar, Kathleen Weil-Garris Brandt, spotted a statue in the lobby of a building that houses the cultural offices of the French Embassy in New York, only footsteps away from The Metropolitan Museum of Art. Having passed the building for years on her way to work at the Institute of Fine Arts, she recognized that the figure of a nude boy standing on a pedestal surrounded by marble columns at the center